MORPH

Accepting,
Embracing,
& Managing Change

By Mark Mayfield
Hall of Fame Speaker & Humorist

TABLE OF CONTENTS

MORPH

Accepting,
Embracing,
and
Managing Change

(This is THE Manual for Change)

INTRODUCTION

Most people are arrogantly passive about change. And by "people", I mean those other guys. I think you're just peachy. And really smart. That's why you're reading this, right?

You must pay attention to change or you will lose control over your destiny. This book can help you have more control over your life.
That's huge.

While there are some givens with change, this writing will have a different twist because it's direct and practical and filled with some actionable items. It also urges the *PROACTIVE* rather than the *REACTIVE* approach to change.
That's huge too.

I'm sure you've noticed this book is small. It's short on word count, but long on content. I like to break things down and make them succinct, and also not intimidate you with an encyclopedia-sized book that would scare you from opening it. So you've got no excuses. Get after it.

OBJECTIVE

My goal with this book is simple. I want to give you
something that will not just help you **survive**
change, but will also help you **thrive** during change.
All that just for the measly price of this book.
I'm that kinda guy.

I'm a firm believer that change is THE metaphor for
life. That's all we do on this planet: **change**. We
are constantly locked in a battle of change, some of
it brought on by us and some brought on by others
or other things. How we respond to those changes
determines the life we lead. Not responding is not a
good option. We must **morph**.

DISCLAIMER

This book will not have footnotes or a bibliography for the simple reason there is only one source: me. And it's not because I'm a special expert on change. We're all experts on change because we all live it. I just happen to be the one chronicling in this book how I have worked through all sorts of change, i.e. loss of a loved one, loss of job, change in relationships, health challenges, paradigm shifts, business trends, technology, etc. Sound familiar? That's because I bet you have dealt with the exact same things.

This book will not be filled with extra verbiage of psycho-babble just so I can make it seem like a more worthy literary effort. It's condensed to make it less confusing, more direct, and to increase the chance of someone reading it. You could even call it a "bathroom book" because one could consume the entire contents fairly quickly, even in one setting. A guy taking his time in the toilet might even be able to read it twice. (And that guy is me.)

Rather than a book, maybe this should be called a manual for managing change (hence the sub-title). I don't care if you refer to it as a manual rather than a book, call it a pamphlet if you like. It doesn't matter to me. I just wanted to write something to break down the change management process and help people through this major stressor of their lives.

So I'm sorry I won't be quoting the results of extensive studies between control groups and variable groups and the numerical assessments from the monitoring and documentation of years of research to a wide variety of change stimuli. Wow, I'm really not sorry. That previous sentence was hard enough to write let alone understand.

Instead, I hope this will be an easy read on one thing you have in common with everybody on earth… change.

I'm not special, I'm just a fallible human like you. Here's what I've learned about change.

Let's begin.

Chapter 1

CHANGE IS HARD

*"If there is no struggle,
there is no progress".*

Frederick Douglass

Change is difficult, but let's be totally honest and destroy a myth. Not all change is hard. If a long lost relative bequeathed you a few million dollars you'd probably be okay with that change in your financial picture. (Coincidentally, a Nigerian Prince is sending me ten million dollars, all I have to do is send him a money order to verify my address. I know, lucky me! #justkidding) But the change that raises our blood pressure is the type of change we generally think of, and which many feel is the majority of change we face. (Actually that's not true, most change is good and makes life better.)

There is change, however, that does shock us and gives us uncertainty, so we have a tendency to put most change into that negative category. And there is angst or skepticism with change innately, because it runs counter to human nature. Everyone's heard the phrase, "we are creatures of habit". Trite and true. The way you comb your hair, answer the phone, or the shoe you put on first is a repeatable habit. Try something for me. Tomorrow morning put the other shoe on first. It will screw up your entire day. Well maybe not, but you'll at least start your day on the wrong foot.
(see what I did there?)

Years ago I heard a speaker say that 72% of all human action was due to "that's the way I've always done it". While I've never been able to verify that statistic, I don't debate it. In fact, it's probably higher. And that's scary...don't think about what you're doing, just meander along on autopilot. It's that type of mindset (or lack thereof) that verifies the fact we are creatures of habit. I bought some apples at the store recently and the clerk asked me if I wanted a sack. I said, "no, just give me a stick and I'll roll them home." He didn't laugh, but why did he ask me for a sack? Habit. No thought. Being a creature of habit is one of the biggest reasons we fight change.

When we're comfortable, it's easier to resist the unknown. Yes, change can be hard, but we make it much harder than it should be because we take the easy route. And we know better. We have an intellectual acceptance to change but a gut resistance. We know we must grow...learn...get better, in other words...change, but it's simpler if we keep on doing what we've always been doing and avoid the sometimes difficult path of change. This I know, if you keep on doing the same things, you will not keep on getting the same results. That's because all the variables and the situation around you will change.

George Bernard Shaw said, "The only man I know who behaves sensibly is my tailor. He takes my measurements anew each time he sees me. The rest go on with their old measurements and expect me to fit them."

Do you want to be happy, succeed, and grow? Then you must continue to evolve.
You must morph.

So how do we get past the fact that some change is hard which leads to our reluctance in positively dealing with it? Here are some tips I think will help you change your mindset, which is the key to this part of change management.

1. *Acknowledge your feelings.* It's okay to be upset or even frightened about a certain change. It's similar to the grieving process in that respect. It doesn't mean you're weak, in fact it just means you're normal. A lot of people are afraid to admit they're struggling with change, but it's okay. So take the necessary time to accept the change, just don't take too long. And don't use this as an excuse to become someone you're not. To morph you must move. Now move on to suggestion 2.

2. *Make a list.* Whatever the change issue, put the "pros" in one column and the "cons" in another, side by side. I love this type of list. They're great reminders. You may have to be a spin-doctor to make sure you don't short change yourself on the "pro" side of your list, so do that if necessary. Get creative and make the "pro" side bigger. Here's an example: I now tell myself it's a good thing to go to the bathroom during the night because I'm getting exercise. It's the same with being forgetful. As I'm wandering around trying to remember what I was looking for, I'm getting exercise. I know, sorta goofy, but this rationalization is a good practice to incorporate into your daily life. Force yourself to find everything positive you can about the change you're dealing with, and then focus on those items. It may be something as simple as, "if this doesn't kill me it'll make me stronger". After you've done that, spend little time reading the "cons", and an abundance of time reading the "pros". Move the positives to the forefront of your mind.

3. *Share.* Talk it out. As you'll see later, a lot of change management is stress management and communication is a great tool in that process. The key here is to talk POSITIVELY about the change. (See suggestion 2)

This first step in the change management phase (acceptance-there's more in chapter 9) is a motivation process. As we all know, the only kind of motivation that is lasting is self-motivation. So I can't help you anymore here. And neither can any great motivational speaker like Tony Robbins. (I actually prefer his brother Baskin for motivation.) Motivation is simply your job. But if you keep having that little voice in your head giving you self-doubt about change and killing your self-motivation, counter those negative thoughts with positive ones from your list. If you still don't think you can change, look at your high school yearbook. HA!

The three "to-do" items I've suggested will hopefully get you past this initial barrier of change. This acceptance phase must happen first. Sad-sack thinking will cause procrastination and stall or even kill change management.

Yep, some change is hard. But we gotta morph on. Suck it up buckaroo.

REVIEW:

Acknowledge change is often difficult.

Make a list of pros and cons.

Talk it out...positively.

Chapter 2

TWO KINDS OF CHANGE

"It's funny how things change slowly until the day we realize they've changed completely."

Nancy Gibbs

Change can be broke down into several pairs of categories like positive/negative, or swift/slow, or mandatory/elective, etc. But those pairings may not be decided by you, so let's focus on the two types of change where you can have some control: change you see coming (expected), and that which you do not (unexpected).

The bottom line is that organically, there is no difference. It's still change. Both will have a response. Both can create stress. Both can be good or bad. Both can be major or insignificant.

The only real difference is time. With change you see coming you have more time. More time to accept it, embrace it, and manage it. More time to plan and adjust. Phones are a good example. Even though phone technology advances have been borderline miraculous, it's been incremental over TIME. Do you remember party lines? You've probably already forgot what a pay phone is? How about those cordless telephones that had the 50-foot retractable antennae? By the time you got that antennae out, the other party had hung up. My neighbor actually convinced me I had to point the antennae in the direction of the party I was speaking to. A real issue if you're geographically challenged. (I wish those two previous sentences were not true).

Bit by bit we morphed with phones. The individual changes may have seemed like a huge leap, but it was much easier because we had the advantage of time. We've generally had that benefit with phones, cars, computers, business practices, and a myriad of other things. This is why even though I'm not a code writer or app developer I've managed to master a host of software programs and can troubleshoot most computer issues. That's because I've had time. I can even take a Selfie. I know. I'm a bragger.

But there are a host of changes that are dramatic and unforeseen. Natural disasters, sudden death, accidents, health issues, unpredictable economic changes, etc. How do we deal with them? The same way as those changes we anticipate, we just have to speed up the timetable. We have less time to accept, embrace, and manage, so we have to morph FASTER.

Obviously this emphasizes the importance of forecasting and planning. If that is done, you can lessen the amount of change that is not anticipated. But whether the change is seen or unseen, it's still just change! You still accept, embrace, and manage...just quicker when time demands. Remember that phrase, it's the theme of this book. *Accept, embrace, and manage.*

REVIEW:

Change is change, whether expected or unexpected.

Planning and forecasting makes change easier.

Unexpected change requires more haste.

Chapter 3

CHANGE IS INEVITABLE

"Change may not be inevitable, but it's definitely unavoidable."

Groucho Marx

As I'll explain in the next chapter, a possible response for you is to just ignore change. Resist and hope it'll disappear. Or maybe crawl in a corner until the change goes away. While that sounds like one of the natural response options (flight), more often than not it doesn't work. It doesn't work because change is inevitable. You can't avoid it. Nor can you wait it out. Sometimes, however, we forget that and think we can just keep on doing what we've always been doing and everything will be just fine. That's folly thinking.

Yes, change is inevitable, I couldn't write anything more un-profound or trite. It's something you can count on, like running into your ex when you look like crap. Why is change automatic? Well let's get basic. Change is a function of time and information. If those two things continue, then change is unavoidable. And quite frankly, you want both of those phenomena to occur. You want information to continue to grow because that's how we solve problems. We learn more. We acquire more information. We want to be smarter tomorrow than we were today. Secondly, we want time to move on because if it stopped,….we'd be dead. That's generally not a good thing. So as long as time and information move on, there will be change.

The variable to this thing called change is speed. Today, change is occurring faster than we ever thought possible. This is why "Change Management" is a paradigm now and will be for a long time. It's due to the speed of change. It's fast now but will be faster yet for the next generation...and the next one....and the next one. My grandfather went from horse drawn equipment to internal combustion engines. Massive change. But it occurred over the span of 80 years. We see that type of dramatic change now in a fraction of that time. Change has always been around and always will be, what's different is the speed of change. It moves at a meteoric pace now.

Since it's not going away, and it's only getting faster, we might as well figure out how to respond to it. Read on.

REVIEW:

Change won't go away...ever.

Change is a function of time and information.

Change will only occur faster, exponentially.

Chapter 4

RESPONSES TO CHANGE

"My washing machine overwhelms me with its options."

Uma Thurman

There are basically three responses to change. The most common option is to just *ignore it*. More people do this than you think. They just ignore the change around them and are stuck in the past refusing to morph. I'm sure you and I both have relatives like this, or we work with someone like this, or, shutter to think...we are like this. These are the people that keep doing the same thing while watching the world pass them by. They put in their 8 to 5, come home, watch the "Wheel of Fortune", drink a six-pack of beer, belch, and go to bed. That's their life. Marching along like robots failing to notice that the world is changing, and doing things because "that's the way I've always done it." When they're asked, "how do you deal with change"? They answer, "I put a cup on the dresser". The only change they deal with is pocket change. This is hyperbole, but I'm trying to make a point. There are multitudes of people who simply ignore change. This is an option. It's generally not a good option, but still an option and probably the most common.

You see people and businesses do this all the time. It's often fatal. Kodak basically ignored the change to digital technology. Sears forgot to update their retail model. Blockbuster Video refused to work with Netflix. These companies failed to morph with the changing marketplace. They ignored it. They kept on doing what they had been doing, not realizing that if you keep on doing what you have been doing, you will not get the results you have been getting. (say that ten times real fast). Those companies mentioned are not the only ones gone or struggling or acquired. Only about 10 percent of the Fortune 500 companies from 1955 even exist today. All of the variables that can create success will change over time, sometimes overnight. Not all change is progress, but certainly all progress is change. Therefore, the only option for continued success is change.

In the interest of full disclosure, if the change has absolutely no connection to you, ignoring it is okay. In fact, you need to do that. Stressing about things that don't really affect you is a waste of time AND unhealthy. But be careful. Items, trends, and demographics that we often think have no bearing on us are few. We are a global society. We are impacted by virtually everything.

The second response to change is to *react*. Just react to what is thrown your way. Sometimes this is the only option afforded us because we couldn't have predicted what was going to happen, but if this is your principal plan...be reactive instead of proactive...the best case scenario for you is second place. You'll never win. You'll be following the crowd just copying their actions and ideas and

23

hoping to sniff some of their success. My dad had a saying when I was growing up, "the head dog is the only sled dog that gets a different view." That's some good southeast Kansas wisdom right there, but it really makes sense when we're talking change. Just reacting to change means you'll always be a step behind. I often think of this when I review what has happened with security screening at airports. From its inception, the TSA has mainly been reacting. Knife attacks...no knives. Shoe bomber...no shoes. Underwear bomber...wow, let's hope they don't go there. Just reacting to change is a good option if all you want to do is exist.

The third option is to *create* change. You initiate the change. You create new ideas, new products, new processes, and you even re-invent yourself. You get better by growing yourself, by changing. By creating change, even with little things, it subconsciously buys you into the change game so that when change is thrown your way by someone or something else, the natural resistance to change is lowered. It sounds like an oxymoron, but the best way to mange change is to create change. If you look at winners in life, you'll often see they were the ones that created new concepts, trends, products, and ideas. They created a new and/or better way. They changed the landscape.

Let's be honest. You'll use all three of these responses. And it's basically summed up in the Serenity Prayer, "God, grant me the serenity to accept the things I cannot change, the courage to change the things I can, and the wisdom to know the difference." It's okay to *ignore* changes in areas that have no effect on your happiness and livelihood. And you will sometimes have to *react* to changes you couldn't see coming. But you'll control your destiny best when you *create* change on your own. Before we figure out how best to do all that, let's understand the correlation between change management and stress management.

REVIEW:

There are three responses to change.

You will employ all three.

Focus on the third response, creating change.

Chapter 5

CHANGE IS STRESSFUL

"Reality is the leading cause of stress among those in touch with it."

Lily Tomlin

Change is stress. Stress is change. And that even goes for good change. You cherish the birth of your child, but with that comes a lot of stress in the ups and downs of caring for them and hoping they have a bright future. Good change and bad change is all very stressful. Experts have slight variations, but all put the following in the list of major stressors in your life:

- Loss of a loved one
- Change in your economic picture
- Change in a relationship
- Addition of a family member
- Career change
- Major health change
- Job responsibility change

Did you notice a word that kept surfacing in that list of stressors? Change. Some are sudden. Some may be planned. Some are excruciatingly painful, but all of them deal with change…major change. If you extend that list out, you would include minor daily changes that can affect your personal life or a business. Those minor changes can be stressful too, so a key aspect of change management is stress management.

I used to believe stress was bogus. Deal with it. Be a man. Toughen up. It's imaginary.

I was an idiot.

Stress is real and it can affect you mentally, emotionally, and physically. I had a doctor tell me once that he believed 75 percent of the people he saw for illness (not injury) had their issue caused by or exacerbated by stress. It's real. Dealing with stress is intertwined with change. Here's why. If you're not operating at peak performance mentally or physically because of stress, it will diminish your ability to deal with the issues of the day...most notably change. Dealing with stress will almost certainly involve a lifestyle change for some, and here are some things that MUST be included.

1. **_Find your moral compass, or your religious beliefs._** Most people know this as a stress management tool. Millions of people came back to their faith after 911. There was a reason for that.

2. **_Move to a more healthy diet._** No information needed here. You know what's good for your body and what's bad. Just be better. You don't have to eliminate the bad (chocolate is one of my basic food groups), just practice moderation.

3. ***Practice a little relaxation.*** Years ago my family physician asked me a question when I came in for health issues that were being magnified by stress. Here's what he asked. "What is the lifespan of a car engine if you run it full tilt all day and night, compared to where you occasionally turn it off and let it cool down." We all know the answer to that question. He told me a body is like an engine in many ways. Every so often, you have to give it a break. I'm not suggesting a three-hour siesta every afternoon (unless you can pull it off, then I wanna work where you do), but get your body into a state of relaxation occasionally. If you don't have the time or money to get to the spa and get that massage, deep breathing is an excellent option. But do it right. Watch a baby. They expand their abdomen and fill their lungs more fully gaining more oxygen transfer. That's a good thing. Adults often suck in their gut and stick out their chest when they deep breathe. We probably started doing that because we look better that way. I know one of the reasons I got married was because I was tired of holding my stomach in. Deep breathing is a cheap, easy, and time efficient way to relax the body. I've always believed one minute of deep breathing an hour is what we should all do. It'll get your heart rate and respiration back where it should be. Can you spare a minute?

4. *Commit yourself to exercise.* The word exercise scares a lot of people because they assume it involves hours out of their day. Not so. You just need a few minutes every day, or as often as you can. Exercise really just needs to satisfy two criteria: make it regular and make it elevate the heart rate. You can see you don't have to be a marathon runner or an NBA basketball player. Using any of the many types of cardio vascular exercise equipment will suffice. I personally prefer the elliptical machine because there are more places to hang clothes after you're done. Kinda wish that weren't true.

5. *Get a hobby.* If I asked you to name your hobby and you can't answer in 10 seconds, you don't have one. Get one. But make sure it is a stress reducer, not a stress inducer. Often, a person's hobby becomes an obsession and then you're defeating the purpose. It needs to be a "getaway" from the issues of the day.

6. *Communicate.* This is why we have friends, family, organizations, and even pets. Pets are great listeners because they don't talk back. They just listen. It's also okay to talk to yourself. (If right now you're asking yourself whether or not you talk to yourself...the answer is yes and that's just fine.) One additional note, there should be one person among your communication partners that you can share ANYTHING with. Even the deepest darkest secret.

It doesn't matter if this is your spouse, pastor, lifelong friend, or daughter, just don't keep anything inside. Share. Keeping issues to yourself is a sure way to move stress to dangerous levels inside your mind and body. Talk it out, or you'll be like a volcano ready to erupt.

7. ***Don't lose your sense of humor.*** This stress reducer is totally free. Doesn't cost a penny. Laughing is a great way to put things in perspective, which is what all of the previously mentioned items can do. It's this simple: you can't laugh and cry at the same time. Totie Fields was a great comedienne of the 60's and 70's. She had a leg amputated and when asked about it said this, "I'd rather lose a leg than lose my sense of humor". Your ability to laugh through tough times makes you more resilient, creative, and stronger. Those are key components in dealing with stress.

Don't pick a couple of these to do. This is not multiple choice. Do them ALL. If you do, you'll prepare your mind and body for the inevitable stress of change that lies ahead.

REVIEW:

Change can be a huge stress.

Manage that stress by relaxing, communicating, exercising, eating right, getting a hobby, laughing, and finding your moral compass.

CHAPTER 6

CREATIVE EXERCISES

"The glass ain't half empty and it's not half full. It's just too big."

George Carlin

Back in chapter four I mentioned you have three responses to change…ignore, react, or create. And I also mentioned some things warrant ignoring or reacting. But this I've witnessed over and over, the people and businesses that are the most successful in surviving and managing change are the ones who predominantly **create** change. You've often heard, "the trend today is…". Well somebody started that trend. Somewhere. Sometime. In short, the entities that are creating the change…
are generally the ones thriving in it. In other words, CREATE, CREATE, CREATE. New ideas, products, processes, and sometimes the situation will even demand that you re-create yourself.

Creativity is often described as finding that "twist" or "perspective" that is not blatantly seen. It's what is NOT obvious. I believe the ability to see that perspective is what creates new things. And some people believe the skill to see that creative angle was only given to a select few like Einstein or Michelangelo, but creativity is innate. Granted some are more gifted than others, but we all have it. If it hasn't surfaced in you, it just needs to be awakened. Here are some great creative exercises to fire up that creative spark inside of you.

1. *Brainstorm.* Formalized by an advertising executive many decades ago, it is still a great idea tool. The key is to not evaluate ideas while you're generating them. Negative thoughts and comments, **and** even positive evaluation can stifle the idea generation process. You can evaluate them later. A good way to do this is to play the "What if" game. What if money, time, and manpower were unlimited? It's amazing how many ideas can be generated when you're not bound with those shackles. You likely will generate some wild ideas, but it's always easier to tame a wild idea than to invigorate a tame one. You also want to think "quantity over quality". The more ideas you have the greater likelihood there is a good one in the batch. It's strictly the law of percentages. So take some time to occasionally brainstorm your issues or problems. Schedule time for this. It's a great creative exercise.

2. ***Join up.*** Human interaction keeps your brain from shutting down. It stimulates your creativity. So get involved in associations or clubs, go to that dinner party, play golf as a foursome instead of by yourself, and suck it up and head to that family reunion even though your creepy Uncle Bert is going to be there with his wife who pinches your cheeks. The mind loves company.

3. *Adopt a questioning attitude.* Ask the question "Why?". When we question what we're doing and why we're doing it, it forces us to evaluate. That improves the odds of finding more creative options. Obviously you want to do this with important personal and business issues, but a good and fun way to practice this is by asking the question "Why" about everyday stuff. Why is there an expiration date on sour cream? (If it goes past that date do you have EXTRA sour cream?) Why do hot dogs come in packages of 10 and hot dog buns come in packages of 8? (Personally I'm tired of buying 40 so it comes out even.) Adopting a questioning attitude can definitely bolster your creativity.

4. *Go into action.* With few exceptions, couch potatoes are not creative geniuses. My experience is that creative people are active people. This doesn't mean you have to be a gym rat, but there is a connection between mental activity and physical activity. The most creative boss I ever reported to had no chairs in his office. He joked that when you sit down you shut off the supply of oxygen to your brain. In his large office he had a workstation shelf along the wall and a standing height table. So take a walk, go to the gym, garden, throw a ball, repair that bike...just move. There is definitely a connection between creativity and action.

5. *Practice Comparison.* Compare what you do with what other successful and happy people do. What positive activities and practices do they employ that you might incorporate into your lifestyle? This is a great exercise for business as well. Sometimes when doing this, businesses make a mistake...they only look inside their industry. People and companies can often incorporate an idea from a very unlikely source outside of their discipline. Fast food restaurants didn't invent the "Drive Thru", banks had employed that for years. Grocery stores didn't invent check-out kiosks, gas stations had been self serve for decades. There are lots of examples like this. Many organizations have an R & D department, which as you know stands for Research and Development. It can also stand for "Rip-off and Duplicate". I'm not saying steal ideas or intellectual property, I'm suggesting keep your eyes open in case you see creative concepts outside of your circle that might work for you.

6. *Play games.* The phrase "use it or lose it" definitely applies to the mind. Exercise your brain. There are an unlimited number of mental games you can buy, or you can just stick with something like the crossword puzzle or Sudoku. Try one and I'll bet you'll find one you like. I personally am a fan of the Rubik's Cube. It forces you to deduce several steps of a problem. And it's also a petroleum based product and burns nicely in the fireplace. HA! Games stimulate the brain.

7. *Hang out with creative people.* There's definitely an osmosis effect when you're with bright and inventive people. The same is true when you're with dull and boring folks. So spend some time with those that engage in lively debate and can make you think. You'll also notice something else. These people are most times upbeat people. I think that's because they see the entire picture. They see all perspectives. Let's be honest, it's much more enjoyable to be with positive people anyway. I remember a management tip I got from one of my first bosses, "If you can't *change* the people around you, then change the *people* around you." He was simply saying spend less time with negative and unimaginative people. Although this might be tough, they could be family. Ugh.

8. *Be a kid.* Have a little fun. One of my favorite sayings is, "You don't stop playing because you grow old, you grow old because you stop playing". Kids haven't had years of rules and restrictions to stifle their creativity. As we age we start self-imposing rules that often don't exist. RULES THAT DON'T EXIST ARE THE WORST KIND OF RULES! This is why I try and spend as much time with my grandkids as I can. They're good for me. They see

things I don't see. They keep me young. These are just some of the questions I've got from young ones lately:

Papa you're old, are you a pilgrim?
Was Humpty Dumpty's mom a great big chicken?
Papa, why is your hair running out of ink?
When you say weed the garden, don't you mean "un-weed"?

9. *Use your sense of humor.* I believe there is a definite connection between your sense of creativity and your sense of humor. I'm not saying one causes the other, I'm saying they enhance one another. The funniest people I know are also incredibly creative. That's because to create comedy you have to find a creative twist that most people don't immediately see. Funny things are often creative things, and creative things are often funny things. And sometimes, you can't tell the difference between the two.

A few years ago, I was in my hotel room getting ready for an engagement when I realized I had forgot to pack dress shoes. It was summer and I had driven my car to this meeting. When I drive in the summer, I drive comfortable. I wear big baggy shorts, a big baggy t-shirt, and these old comfy white loafers. As I'm getting ready to go on stage,

I realize these white loafers are the only shoes I have with me. I have a dark double-breasted suit and white shoes. I look sassy! No I don't. I look like an idiot. I panicked, went downstairs, and tried to cajole the bellman out of his shoes. (I used the word "cajole" here to give you a word to look up in the dictionary. You can get extra credit for this. Go ahead, do this now so you know the correct definition and pronunciation. Okay, let's continue.)

I had no luck cajoling him out of his shoes. He did, however, inform me of a clothing store across the street that carried shoes. I didn't have time to race upstairs and change, so I ran into this clothing store wearing a dark suit and white shoes. It was like Pat Boone making a comeback. (This metaphor is for you old fogies who remember Pat Boone.) As I entered through the door, I looked at the storeowner and asked, "What do you suppose I need?" His answer was quick: "A white suit?"

My first impression was that this guy was very funny, but when you think about it, he's much more than that. While I certainly admire his wit, it's his creativity that will put more money in his pocket. He knows the margin or profit on selling me a suit is far greater than on a pair of shoes. This guy was not a comedian, but he had a trait that great comedians have. He had the ability to see "the other alternative". He was creative. I've never met a great comedian who wasn't also really creative. Your sense of humor and your sense of creativity are almost synonymous.

You may have noticed. This tip is also a stress management tool I mentioned in an earlier chapter. That's because the ability to see alternatives is the core of creativity, and it's also what helps you see the big picture, which keeps things in perspective. So laugh it up. Lighten up. You want to enhance your creativity, use your sense of humor. And you'll also get a stress management benefit too.

REVIEW:

Becoming more creative or "vibrant" helps you through change.

The mind: use it or lose it.

Sharpen your mind by doing creative exercises.

CHAPTER 7

THE PEOPLE FACTOR

"You are unique, like everyone else."

Margaret Mead

This is a critical factor when it comes to embracing and thriving during change. Managing change is not a game of solitaire. Change is a human thing and a team thing. We often only see the technology or demographic side of change, but it's people that cause the change and are the conduit for working through it. In other words, if your people skills are weak your change management skills are correspondingly weak. People help you through the problems and stressors of life. As Alex Haley said, "if you see a turtle on top of a fence post, you know he had some help". Let's face it, change is just a problem...a challenge. You use people to help you through other problems, why not let them help you through change?

For years I've told audiences one of the best ways to enhance your people skills is to follow the Golden Rule. Not the one you learned in Sunday School, most of us know and follow that one. We need to also follow the Golden Rule of Human Relationships. It goes like this, "Do Unto Others As They Want To Be Done Unto". In other words, treat people the way they want to be treated. Recognize differences and respond accordingly.

You're going to need people to get through the vagaries of change. That means you need to understand people and shift when you have to.

That's the point behind all of those social style and personality assessment programs. I've been through most of them and certified to teach a few. What I've found is that I'm a squiggly line, orange, dominant, jerk. Very helpful. My buddy, George Campbell, even does one using characters from Gilligan's Island. You're either a Gilligan, the Skipper, Mr. Howell, or the Professor. And if you think that's stupid, you're a Professor. Regardless of what assessment program you subscribe to, the takeaway is to determine and respect a person's style. Shift, move, and be flexible. You need them on your team. Teamwork is key in marching through change. If you're dealing with someone who is fast paced, cut-to-the-chase, and a "get 'er done" person, then you need to try and be fast paced, cut-to-the-chase, and get 'er done. But that's not always the case. You may be dealing with someone who is slower paced, more sensitive, and they may want to talk about Aunt Myrtle's prostate surgery (just a check to see if you're actually reading this). In that case, you'll need to slow down, shift, and emulate them more. One of the key learning points of those programs is to mirror people a little bit to get them on your side. Make them comfortable. Build a rapport. You need people on your side if you're going to navigate change.

This is obviously easier for some than it is for others. Some folks can get along with anybody, others mirror a quote from Charles Schulz, "I love mankind. It's people I can't stand". We've all felt that way at one time or another because people can be morons. But with regard to change, we need to put aside some differences and partner up. This is not an option. Change is a team game.

REVIEW:

People help you through change.

Being flexible is one of the greatest people skills.

CHAPTER 8

STAY POSITIVE

"Be positive, a day without sunshine is, you know, night".

Steve Martin

Despite all the wisdom and information imparted in this book (I just dislocated my shoulder patting myself on the back), there will be days when you say, "no, I can't do this". This will mean you're normal. Change can be overwhelming at times, but believe in yourself. Stay positive.

That's why this will be the shortest chapter in this book, but the most valuable. Just know: YOU CAN CHANGE, BECAUSE YOU HAVE!

Humans are very adaptive creatures. You have been morphing your entire life but you often forget that. You don't think you can change? Have a baby! Parents figure out real quick just how adaptive they are. You are far better at change than you think. Change is just growing up, and it's normal to make a lot of mistakes in that process. (Anybody else go through the leisure suit and platform shoes phase?)

So don't worry if you struggle a little bit. Go ahead, screw up. Then forgive yourself and remind yourself, "I got this".

You can change...because you have your entire life.

REVIEW:

Stay positive.

Self-talk through change.

CHAPTER 9

PHASES OF CHANGE

"An egg can't fly, but the bird inside it eventually can."

Anonymous

Anonymous is my favorite author. He (or she) wrote a lot of great things. Of all the things attributed to Anonymous, this one about the egg and the bird may be my favorite. Much better than which came first, or why one crossed the road. The reason I love this quote is because it sums up the phases of change: accept, embrace, and thrive. It's called growth, or....morphing.

I wrote some helpful tips on accepting change in chapter one. If you're still struggling with that, go back for a review. You've got to get through that first or it will hamper the next two phases. Each phase can have varying durations, but that's principally up to you. And I repeat, if you are in a constant state of denial and never accept change, the two phases after that never occur.

This was my initial problem with technology. I didn't accept it. For the longest time I believed the Internet was a fad. Why wouldn't I? My basement was filled with boxes of 8-track tapes and cases of cassette tapes. For you youngsters who have no idea what I'm talking about, here's a brief synopsis. An 8-track tape was the size of a dictionary that you placed into a device the size of a microwave. This left no legroom for the driver or the passenger if you drove anything smaller than a Mack Truck. There were really only four tracks and the reels of this archaic equipment created a squeaky and grinding noise that would become the inspiration for Grunge music. It was a great invention. (Sarcasm font needed). The 8-track was replaced with the smaller cassette tape that one out of four times was eaten by the cassette player and required a surgical procedure to remove the quarter-inch tape wrapped around the heads. If you were somehow successful with that endeavor, you had to take a pencil, insert it into the spokes of the reel, and attempt to recoil the mangled tape. This worked approximately one in a million times. In short, I had been duped into believing technology was a good thing only to see those inventions have the lifespan of a Mayfly (they live about 24 hours in case you're not an entomologist). I wasn't going to fall for this again. Computers and the Internet were just another conspiracy. I was sure of it.

I was just a little wrong. (Sarcasm font needed again.)

Because I took so long in the acceptance phase, I was way behind the curve in the embrace phase. Embracing change means planning and learning. It means REALLY making a commitment. It's not just saying, "I need to do this sometime" or "I really ought to get on that". To embrace change you have to set a timetable and stick to it. For me and technology, that meant actually forking out some cash and allocating time to learn it. So I had my brother Elton (the IT guru and "first adopter" of the family) make me a list of everything I needed to get started. His list included things and descriptions that were totally foreign to me at the time: mega-giga-biting things, software, hardware, casual ware, Tupperware....I was totally lost. And he had me get a host of drives, adaptors, cables and other accessories that I was sure he had just made up to embarrass me into asking for them at the store. "Where do I find the bi-polar, coagulating, slippage connector?"

Marching through the electronics store I loaded up my shopping cart with technology that would make me a techno-wiz. During checkout I stopped the clerk in mid-scan. "Pardon me miss, is this mouse pad compatible with this computer?" (I wish I was making this part up.) She was much more savvy than her years implied and saw this as a rare comedic opportunity. "I honestly don't know", she said. "That's way above my pay grade. We need to call in Tech Support for this one". She then called someone named "Charlie" and told him to bring all the technicians over because they didn't want to miss this question. I didn't catch on and soon asked seven geeks the same question. Here's something you should know. That's funny stuff in Geek Land.

My delay in accepting the change of technology caused a further delay in embracing what this could actually mean for me. After fully embracing this change (planning and learning), I now am fully into the "thriving" aspect of technology change. In fact, I now wonder how I ever got along without cell phones, computers, software, and the myriad of technological advances that make running my business and career possible. In fact, it's reached a point where learning new software or a piece of technology is actually fun. But I do still wonder...what about that mouse pad question?

Notice at this stage in the book, I used the word "thrive" instead of "manage". The word "manage" can sometimes have an implication of just getting by. That's not the goal. Get so good at managing change that you're not just existing, you're thriving. Make change work for you.

But remember, don't forget the order. The landscape of change is littered with individuals and companies that only partially accepted or embraced change before they jumped into it. Accept and embrace comes first. Commit to those two things fully, and you significantly increase your chance to thrive.

REVIEW:

The phases of change are accept, embrace, and thrive.

A delay in the first two phases delays your ability to thrive.

The phases have to be done in sequence.

CHAPTER 10

TIMING

"Make haste slowly."

Carl Jung

When change comes easy for you....it's often too late. When people or companies fail so badly or get so far behind they finally embrace change, the ship may have already sunk. Show me a company or individual changing during good times, and I'll show you longevity of success. Whether it's a business or a relationship, it's tough to un-sink a ship.

This means you have to morph and often you have to morph FAST.

I'm not a car guy, or "gearhead" as they are sometimes referred. My brother loved tinkering with mechanics so I let him do that sort of stuff growing up. I just don't really care about cars. I drive a little crappy compact. I bought it because the dealer said it would stop on a dime. The reason: it can't get over the dime. The cigarette lighter and the heater are the same device. I turn my radio on and the car slows down. Okay, that's an old stand-up bit and I don't drive a compact, but I really don't put much priority on a car. So I know little when it comes to taking care of them. I know this has cost me money over the years. My mechanic charged me $82 to sharpen my lug nuts last week (sorry, more of the old bit). So it may seem odd how I ended up driving a Formula 1 race car on an official track one day. Long story, but basically I was speaking to a group of people in the morning who spent the afternoon on the track and they wanted me to be part of the racing experience. I feigned interest because they paid me to speak. I was a capitalist way before I was a speaker.

My trepidation for being part of this process was two fold. First, while most men would pee their pants when offered the opportunity to drive a race car, it just didn't appeal to me. As I mentioned, I don't' really care about cars. Secondly, to perform this little exercise they made you wear a fire retardant suit. Here's a common sense observation. If the activity in which you are about to partake requires a fire retardant suit, I'm gonna suggest it's a bad activity. Nonetheless, with about five seconds of instruction, we hit the track.

You follow a professional driver and the amateurs take turns being the lead driver behind the pro. Eventually it was my turn to lead and after going so slow I created a traffic jam on the track, the professional driver motioned me off the track. Another pro met me and suggested I stop driving in first gear. Good information. I thought I only had one gear. On the straight portion of the track, I had it maxed out in full throttle. Kinda loud. It was a week before my ears stopped ringing. He then told me I was not letting the car dynamics function as they should because I was driving too slow. He informed me the spoiler, for example, was like an airplane wing. A wing on an airplane causes lift, but if you flip it upside down it creates down force. He told me I needed to speed up to make features like this work, he said I needed to **accelerate through the curve**. That's right. He told me to speed up through the turns.

At this point I had been thoroughly embarrassed. All the other drivers were laughing each time they passed. Some were giving me the one finger salute. So I got back on the track and when it was my time to lead, I figured what the heck, I'm going all out. After all, I'm wearing a fire retardant suit, right?

I came into the first turn and simply floored it and an amazing thing happened. The car literally hugged the road. It became more stable. I had more control. The faster I went, the easier it seemed to drive and at this point I became a complete idiot. I couldn't go fast enough. I even used all the gears. And I'm proud to say that as of this writing, I'm the only amateur driver in the history of that driving school to pass the professional driver. It was pretty simple. Just drafted for a lap, gave him a bump stop, took him on the inside...he didn't have a chance. I should also say I am the only guy to be told to leave the track and not come back.

There are a million metaphors for change, but maybe none better than *"accelerate through the curve"*. When change hits us we often hesitate, push back, and slow down. In the race of life, that gives everyone a chance to pass us by. I'm certainly not saying we charge ahead without doing due diligence, but avoid the temptation of going too slow. One of the best books I ever read was, "It's Not the Big That Eat the Small...It's the Fast That Eat the Slow". In this rapid world of change, we have to speed up. Take your time, but do it quickly.

REVIEW:

Change during good times as well as bad.

Don't be afraid to pick up the pace.

Accelerate through the curve.

CHAPTER 11

CHANGE =
PROBLEM SOLVING

"Problem solving is hunting. It is savage pleasure and we are born to it."

Thomas Harris

I'm a simple-minded guy (insert your joke about me, I can handle it). That's why I like the statement, "If you're a good problem solver, you can handle change." That's basically what I'm talking about in this book...being a good problem solver.

Change can upset the apple cart. It can cause problems. In fact, any item of change can be viewed as a problem. Hence, good problem solvers are good change managers. And problems aren't necessarily a bad thing. In fact most problems are a by-product of success. Look at it this way: when you solve a problem you've created a new scenario. With that comes new issues or problems to deal with or...change. Solve those issues and guess what, another new scenario and a new set of problems.

I'm not trying to rationalize too much, but problems can be a very good thing. It often means we've been successful at something. In short, I'm saying we want new problems, not old problems that we work on for years that never go away. That shows a lack of success. As we all know, we've got many of those in the world. Some are centuries old...that's a significant unwillingness to change.

If we become better problem solvers, we also become better change managers. Here are my eight steps to problem solving.

1. ***Attitude.*** I'm probably scaring you here and truly, I write this hesitantly. Why? Because many people believe all you have to do is have a good attitude. Some motivational speakers even preach this. "If you believe it you can achieve it." Horse hockey. Here's my point: attitude is the most important thing because it's step number one but it's not the only thing. If all you have is a good attitude you'll be the happiest loser on your block. Things will suck for you but you'll smile and keep charging ahead into one disaster after another. For example, growing up I rode horses nearly every day. I had a dream of winning the Kentucky Derby. I could have been an excellent jockey. I was 4'11" and weighed 96 pounds as a sophomore in high school. I've got an old drivers license to prove it. In college my body discovered hormones. I'm 6' and weigh 190 pounds now. Despite all my positive attitude and belief in myself, I'll never be a world-class jockey. Not unless we start racing Clydesdales. Attitude is the first thing you have to do, but it's worthless without the following seven steps.

2. ***Define the problem.*** This may be the most critical step, for if we don't have a clear handle on the REAL issue, we have no chance of fixing it PERMANENTLY.

Many times we don't define the problem, we focus on a symptom of the problem. When that happens, you're just putting a Band-aid on the issue. Years ago at a function I was attending, a gentlemen had a mild heart attack. But we didn't know that because he only complained of a bad headache and indigestion. So we gave him Tylenol and Tums. Did we treat the problem? No, we only treated the symptoms because we didn't accurately define the problem. Make sure you get to the real issue at hand and that may require digging deep into the problem.

3. *Generate ideas.* This is a simple brainstorm exercise. Get lots of options on the table. Explore. Get creative. The key as I've mentioned before in this book, is to not evaluate these thoughts. This step is solely to get ideas on the table.

4. *Evaluate ideas.* Notice how step four comes after step three. Evaluating ideas during the generation step will STOP the generation process. Don't evaluate until you're sure the idea generation step has run its course.

5. *Make a decision.* You've evaluated, now weigh the pros and cons and make a call.

6. ***Develop a plan.*** Choose a course of action. Get your strategy together.

7. ***Action.*** Do it. Jump right in and commit to your plan.

8. ***Evaluate the problem***. Did you fix it or did you not? If the problem persists you've had a breakdown in one of the previous steps. Was your attitude less than committed? Did you define the problem wrong? Did you not generate enough ideas to fix the problem? etc., etc.

The aforementioned problem solving process only applies to a few types of problems: personal, professional, emotional, economic, private, and public. (If you've got a problem outside of these categories, please let me know, it'll be a first in the history of mankind.)

And also, you already do this problem solving process. You know it, maybe subconsciously, but you do. It's innate. Did you know on simple tasks like changing the temperature of the water in your shower, you go through all these steps? Almost simultaneously, but you zip through all steps to get the temperature just right. Here's the catch, as the problems become more complex the more regimented you must be in making sure each step is finished before moving on. On major issues, months can be spent on a single step. Follow these steps and change will get easier for you. In other words, be a better problem solver and you'll be better at coping with change. I promise you.

REVIEW:

Solving the riddle of change is really just solving problems.

Follow my eight steps of problem solving.

CHAPTER 12

SO NOW WHAT?

"Failure is not fatal. Failure to change might be."

John Wooden

As I've mentioned, I'm putting change into two categories...expected and unexpected. Often the unexpected change is bad, even horrific. But if you are constantly morphing, when something is thrown in your lap you are more likely to accept, embrace, and thrive. In other words, you can acclimate yourself to change by constantly changing. It sounds like an oxymoron, but to manage change you must create change. You can start small. Rearrange the furniture. Take a different route to work. Order something different from the menu. Just get accustomed to change. Who knows, after a while you may be learning a second language or writing a book. (What do you think started this book?) Make change a normal part of your life so you're not upended when change is thrown your way. Because it will happen! Take change by the hand or it'll get you by the throat. And oh yeah, if you get better at managing change it'll make you better at your job and more fun to be around.

So there's that.

And remember what I mentioned earlier. We often have a tendency to only change when we're forced to. That's a dangerous route. Change during bad times AND during good times.

Finally, you may have some confusion over the three responses to change versus the three phases of change. To be blunt, they intersect. For example, ignore change (a response) and you're assured of never accepting change (a phase). Or make a commitment to create change (a response) and you significantly increase your chance of thriving during change. The response you choose can very likely determine your phase. And as you can tell, I strongly encourage you to create change as often as you can so you can thrive during change...
the ideal phase.

Okay, one more thing.

This will get harder as you get older. That's a fact of life. I know you've heard the phrase, "you can't teach an old dog new tricks". (Does that mean you **can** teach them **old** tricks?) The older we get the more regimented we become. This is why I believe kids are more resilient than adults. One moment it's the end of the world for them, the next minute they're on top of it. They adapt and change far better than us old folks. So be aware of this. It doesn't mean you can't change as you age, it just means you have more reluctance. So...

MORPH. NOW.

SUMMARY

For those of you who want the bullet points of the
cliff notes version of a summary of the abbreviated
copy of this short book, here it is.

- Change is hard but inevitable. Suck it up.

- Don't tell me you can't change, you've been doing it
your entire life.

- There are three responses to change:
Ignore. React. Create.

- There are three phases of change:
Accept. Embrace. Thrive.

- To manage change the best, you must create
change...constantly. Start with little things.

- You can be more creative. Exercise your mind.

- Change is often stressful. Practice stress
management.

- Good problem solvers are good change managers.

- Have fun. It helps your creativity, which helps you
manage stress and manage change.

MY TO-DO LIST:

Studies show that if you write it down you have a much better chance of getting something done. Use this page to make notes to yourself about changes you've been thinking about, but just haven't got around to doing. Just do it.

MORPH.

Now we're done.
Stop whining and get going.

(That sentence was from my mom,
 she's always had the last word.)

To contact Mark Mayfield about speaking at your event or for more information about his programs or any of his materials, please use the contact information below:

Mark Mayfield
mark@markmayfield.com
816-532-8702

There will be no sixteen prompts or a call center if you dial that number. Unless he's on stage or in the shower (or on the golf course), you'll talk to him directly.

You can also learn more about Mark and see him in action at:

www.markmayfield.com